At last! A program that teaches everyone skills to stop and think.

— **Ricardo Esparza, Ph.D.**
Cross-Cultural Clinical Psychologist

This is a terrific little book that helps parents become more mindful of their parenting and helps children think before they act.

— **David Olds, Ph.D.**
Professor of Pediatrics and Director,
Prevention Research for Family and Child Health,
University of Colorado, Denver

Want to sharpen your thinking skills and make better decisions? Dr. Barry has translated new findings about how the brain works into an easy-to-read book that will help you use your wise or "Wizard Brain" and make good choices.

— **Nicole B. Sperekas, Ph.D.**
Author of several books for parents and children

Other books by Patricia Gorman Barry, Ph.D.

BRAINWISE FOR GRADES K–5
(A curriculum of scripted lesson plans and
reproducible student worksheets)

BRAINWISE FOR GRADES 6–12
(A curriculum of scripted lesson plans and
reproducible student worksheets)

BRAINWISE ONE-ON-ONE
(A curriculum for counselors, social workers, nurses,
and others who work with individuals; contains scripted
lesson plans and reproducible student worksheets)

How To Be BrainWise®

The Proven Method for Making Smart Choices

How To Be BrainWise®

The Proven Method for Making Smart Choices

Patricia Gorman Barry, Ph.D.

Innisfree Press
Denver, Colorado

For information, write to this address:
BrainWise®
c/o Innisfree Press
P.O. Box 8375
Denver, CO
80201-8375

www.howtobebrainwise.com

ISBN: 0-9748764-4-5

Printed in Canada

Table of Contents

Preface

*Every time a man stands for an ideal, or acts to improve
the lot of others, or strikes out against injustice, he sends
forth a tiny ripple of hope . . . those ripples build a current that
can sweep down the mightiest walls of oppression and resistance.*
—Robert F. Kennedy

This quote has been above my desk for many years. A good friend, now deceased, sent it to me the first year I began teaching the thinking skills that now are called the BrainWise program. Walls of oppression and resistance may be of our own doing, or they may be built by others. Either way, we need tools to understand problem situations and learn how to prevent or solve them.

How To Be BrainWise: The Proven Method for Making Smart Choices gives you what you need to make better choices and decisions. This book summarizes concepts we successfully have taught in schools, agencies, and businesses throughout the world. Also called critical thinking, the ten skills help you learn how to stop and think before you react.

Just as the letters of the alphabet form a foundation for reading, the 10 Wise Ways form a foundation for thinking. They are presented in simple terms, making them easy to remember, practice, and teach to others.

This framework will help you understand wisdom and how to attain it. Please share these skills. The best way to learn is by teaching others.

Acknowledgments

I want to thank Drs. Aaron Beck, Albert Bandura, Herbert Benson, Megan Gunner, Richard Jessor, Eric Kandel, David Olds, Bruce Perry, Robert Sternberg, and Bessel van der Kolk whose research and publications about the brain, behavior, education, children, teenagers, parents, and adults helped me understand the thinking process.

Dr. Nicki Sperekas, Dr. Marilyn Welsh, Ed Rogers, Steven Silvers, Virginia Castro, Dr. Ricardo Esparza, Dr. Jillian Jacobellis, Thomas Balance, Jewell Dean Underwood, Dr. David Cooper, Rep. Terrance Carroll, and Pauline Haberman believed in the BrainWise program. Their support was and is invaluable.

Wendy Cameron, Marsha Harman, Karen Senier, Pat Austin, Flavia Lewis, Michael Dean, Nancy Wilson, Barb Lamana, Tracy Dodd, Tim La Greca, Matt Sena, Ed Isley, Brenda Brown, Julee Heit, Judy Cardenas, Valerie Silvers, Karen McCaman, Rathski Hamid, Brenda Knoop, and Jody Huntington represent the legions of outstanding instructors who have helped showcase BrainWise. They taught me that a curriculum is as good as the person teaching it. Pam Buckley not only is a gifted teacher; her dedication and talent helped BrainWise get off the ground.

Many generous donors and foundations supported the development and distribution of the BrainWise curricula. They include Robert McKenzie, the Audrey K. Dines Memorial Fund, the Donnell-Kay Foundation, the Adolph Coors

Foundation, the Hunt Alternatives Fund, the Cloverleaf Foundation, the Denver Foundation, the Junior League of Denver, the Rose Community Foundation, American Family Insurance, WB2 Charities, the Daniels Fund, the Colorado Women's Foundation, Bill Rosser and Karen Westrill, Randy Holman Productions, Henry Gill Advertising, and TyL.

Don Eberle taught me the importance of practicing what you preach.

Brigid Gorman Barry taught me the 10 Wise Ways and showed me how to live them.

Everyone Has Problems

Difficulties mastered are opportunities won.
— Winston Churchill

Have you ever said to yourself, "Why did I just do that? What on earth was I thinking?" Maybe you've found yourself getting possessive about "your" stretch of the road. Perhaps you've engaged in an argument that exploded into a war of words, or worse. Or maybe you've stormed out of a room in a fit of anger or frustration or have been so excited that you babbled like an idiot. If so, welcome to the human race.

None of us is perfect. From the president whose affairs make headlines to the friend who does not take the car keys away from a buddy who has had too much to drink, we all do things we later regret.

Why? Why do we at times react emotionally rather than respond rationally?

The answer lies in the brain, the way it's wired, and the short-circuiting that occurs when we don't stop to think.

This book makes it easy to understand the brain and why people act the way they do. It distills findings from research and proven techniques in medicine, education, and the social sciences and presents them as concepts termed the "10 Wise Ways." Each chapter introduces a wise way and explains how it is part of the problem-solving process.

If the letters of the alphabet are a reading tool, the 10 Wise Ways are a thinking tool. Like letters, these concepts are easy to remember, but knowing them does not mean you know how to think, any more than knowing the alphabet means you automatically know how to read. You use the wise ways to learn how to think in the same way you use letters to learn to read.

You depended on your family and other adults to teach you how to think. If you were raised in a family or an environment where people hadn't learned thinking skills, or had learned them incompletely, you probably grew up without learning important problem-solving strategies.

Until now, this information has been a well-kept secret — not because people who know about thinking skills won't share them, but because people who have learned how to make good choices and decisions are unaware that they learned skills others have not. They do not realize that people who respond using emotions and impulse are acting on basic "fight or flight" instincts, the only response they know. *How To Be BrainWise* lets you in on this "secret." The 10 Wise Ways will teach you how to stop and think, helping you make better choices so you have fewer problems. This book will help you quickly grasp these techniques and use them in your everyday life. Better yet, you will have tools to teach these important skills to others.

The ideas BrainWise presents are universal and can be applied to any problem situation. You already may know or be familiar with many thinking skills. This book will help you understand how they work, why they are important, and how you can incorporate thinking into your responses to everyday life.

Today, ways to prevent problems are not systematically taught at home and school. The BrainWise program has given thousands of parents, educators, counselors, social workers, mentors, clergy, and health professionals methods to teach the skills necessary to stop and think. They have found the techniques useful for everyone, regardless of sex, race, age, or culture.

As with all learned skills, the more you use them, the better you become. It takes practice to master thinking, but soon you will automatically stop and think before you react. This *AHA!* experience will make your life at home, work, and school happier, healthier, and more productive.

Wise Way #1: Using Your Wizard Brain Over Your Lizard Brain

If there is a way to do it better ... find it.
— Thomas Edison

Despite what the poets may say, emotions do not spring from the human heart. They — like thoughts — are centered in the brain, thus setting up the classic conflict of human nature: emotion versus reason. To better learn how to respond rationally rather than react emotionally, it helps to understand how the brain works.

Your five senses — taste, touch, sight, smell, and sound — are not designed merely to experience pain or pleasure. They have a purpose. The senses act as the body's guards, sending signals to your brain and alerting it to protect you from harm.

The Thalamus — The Brain's Relay Center

The senses send signals to an area in the middle of your brain called the thalamus.* It acts as a relay center. When your senses send an urgent message, the thalamus automatically relays the warning to the limbic system, triggering survival responses.

---

*Smell does not send signals to the thalamus but to a nearby area of the brain.

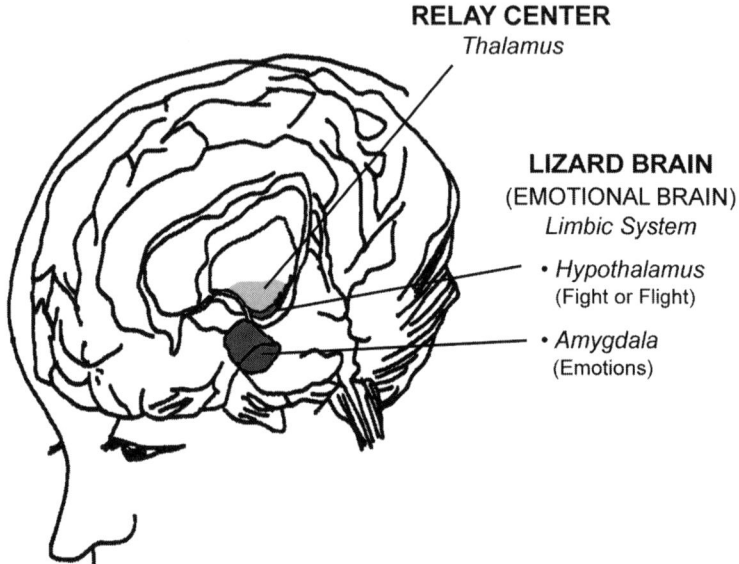

RELAY CENTER
Thalamus

LIZARD BRAIN
(EMOTIONAL BRAIN)
Limbic System

• *Hypothalamus*
  (Fight or Flight)

• *Amygdala*
  (Emotions)

The Limbic System — The Lizard Brain

The limbic system is located just below the thalamus, in the lower back of your head, above your neck.

The limbic system includes two important sections: the hypothalamus ("hypo" means underneath) and the amygdala. The hypothalamus contains and releases the "fight or flight" instinct. This survival response is found even in reptiles, giving the limbic system its more descriptive name, Lizard Brain.

The amygdala is the source of emotions. The emotion most critical to survival is fear. The Lizard Brain does not differentiate among fear, anger, revenge, greed, lust, hate, jealousy, love, excitement, or any other feeling — positive or negative. This part of the brain perceives all intense emotions as fear and reacts to them as threats.

Everyone is born with the Lizard Brain's survival system. When you touch a hot flame, your hand pulls back automatically. When you taste something awful, you spit it out. When a siren goes off, you seek safety. You back away from a vicious dog and you flee when you smell gas.

The Lizard Brain does not stop to think about warning signals; it reacts to them. This response is key to survival, and it was especially handy a thousand or more years ago when society was less civilized.

Today, we seldom encounter life-threatening events. Even though society has changed, the Lizard Brain has not. It continues to interpret all intense emotions as threats, triggering numerous "survival mode" responses in your body. Your heart beats faster; your muscle tone alters; and various chemicals shoot through your body, preparing it to react quickly and impulsively.

Today, those reactions are used not to frighten or escape from an attacking bear, but to show road rage or engage in some other form of nonthinking behavior. The brain perceives threats to egos in the same way it perceives life-threatening events.

If you ever have found yourself asking, "What was I thinking?" or "What were they thinking?", here's your answer: You were not thinking — no one was. Your Lizard Brain simply was reacting to emotions it perceived as threats, even though no danger was involved, only intense feelings of anger, excitement, surprise, or other strong emotions.

You, like everyone else, were born with your senses hardwired to send signals to the thalamus and on to the Lizard Brain. You were not born with the ability to screen your senses and the intense emotions they elicit. Neither were you born with the ability to analyze whether reacting impulsively to a situation is a good response.

Analysis occurs in another part of the brain — the prefrontal cortex, which is located behind the forehead. In this book, we refer to the prefrontal cortex as the Wizard Brain. It is the source of wisdom.

The Wizard Brain

People who experience fewer problems in life have learned to use thinking skills to bypass Lizard Brain reactions. The remainder of this book discusses the thinking process and shows how you, too, can make your Wizard Brain work for you.

The Wizard Brain is where problem-solving takes place. It is where you stop and think before you react.

Although we are born with our thalamus connected to the Lizard Brain, no one is born with connections linking the thalamus and Lizard Brain to the Wizard Brain. You create these connections only when you learn skills that help you realize, "Hey! I better stop and think about this!" before reacting. The 10 Wise Ways of using your Wizard Brain over your Lizard Brain are the skills that allow you to make those new connections.

You now are aware that reacting impulsively and responding wisely take place in two different sections of your brain. You also know that the brain is designed to react — and it always will do so unless you have learned skills to help it stop and think.

Lizard Brain reactions underlie problems ranging from seeking attention by throwing a temper tantrum to causing an accident because of road rage. They also are why people are "crazy in love" or so excited they lose control and tear down the goalposts.

The good news is that thinking skills can be learned. Every time you become aware of and practice a thinking

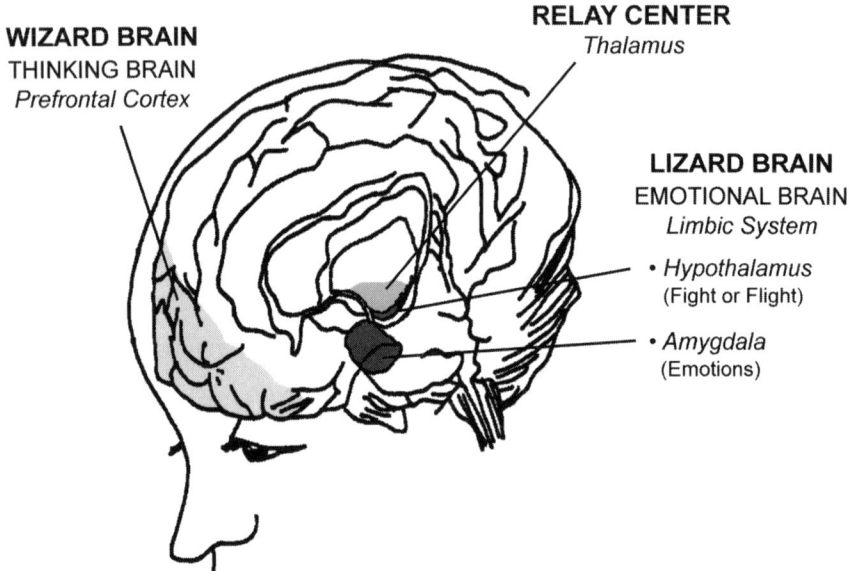

WIZARD BRAIN
THINKING BRAIN
Prefrontal Cortex

RELAY CENTER
Thalamus

LIZARD BRAIN
EMOTIONAL BRAIN
Limbic System

• *Hypothalamus*
(Fight or Flight)

• *Amygdala*
(Emotions)

skill, you are building connections from your thalamus to your Wizard Brain. Practice makes these connections stronger, creating a network of pathways linking your thinking brain to its survival system. (Speaking of survival, sex drive is also found in the Lizard Brain.)

Building new connections in your brain is called "neuroplasticity." Showing how this process works earned Eric Kandel, M.D., the 2000 Nobel Prize in Medicine. Neuroplasticity refers to the ability of neurons (cells of the nervous system) to form new connections through the brain's cortex. If you think of neurons as wires, you would call it "rewiring the brain." You will learn how to put this exciting knowledge into practice by using your Wizard Brain over your Lizard Brain, in conjunction with nine other skills.

Together, these 10 Wise Ways will help you build connections to your thinking brain. The process helps you and your brain form a solid foundation of skills so you learn how to stop and think in virtually any situation.

With practice, you will become aware that thinking helps you control your emotions and impulses. When this happens, it is a wonderful *AHA!* experience.

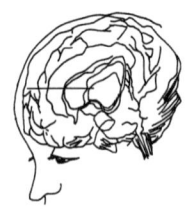 **Build a Brain Connection**

After you learn about a Wise Way or thinking skill, picture in your mind that you are building a neural pathway connecting both your brain's relay center and Lizard Brain to your Wizard Brain. From now on, after you learn about each thinking skill, you will be asked to make a "brain connection." Your first connection is being aware of your thinking Wizard Brain and emotional Lizard Brain.

The connection will be weak at first but becomes stronger with practice. (Remember that the skill disappears if it is not used and will quickly be replaced by Lizard Brain reactions.) To gain practice, do the following:

- Identify impulsive and emotional behaviors and distinguish them from wise choices made by thinking.

- Practice by assessing current events and the behaviors you observe around you, on television and in movies, at work — everywhere — as a Lizard Brain or a Wizard Brain response. Be sure to include your own behaviors as well as those of others.

- With practice, Wizard Brain thinking can be just as fast as Lizard Brain reactions. Practice recognizing this "quick thinking" and distinguishing it from impulsive and emotional Lizard Brain responses. Quick thinkers are experts at applying and using thinking skills.

- Who do you know who has only a few problems? Who do you know who has many problems? Think about how they respond to problems and which brain they use.

AHA! Experience
[Chris, mother]

AS THE PARENT OF A TEENAGER, I worry. Every year teenage deaths from car accidents and alcohol poisoning make local headlines. I never understood how kids who have had a good driver's education course and who know about the dangers of driving too fast, not wearing seat belts, and drinking and driving could make such fatal choices. Now I realize how strong a hold the Lizard Brain's impulse and emotion have on them and how it underlies the faulty thinking of even "smart" kids.

This awareness was an AHA! moment for me. I have made sure that my son understands how his Lizard Brain can take over when he is around his friends, and that it is the only brain being used by someone who is under the influence of drugs or alcohol.

[Karyn, artist and mother]

MY AHA! EXPERIENCE HAPPENED when I forgot to buckle my seat belt. My five-year-old was learning BrainWise in school and said, "Mom, you're using your Lizard Brain!" I realized that she understood an important concept and was teaching it to me.

[Sam, construction worker]

AT WORK, WE LEARNED ABOUT THE DIFFERENCE *between using your Wizard Brain and Lizard Brain. It is funny how something so simple can help you stop and think, but it has helped all of us pay attention to how we practice safety and has helped prevent some serious injuries.*

[Jewell, businesswoman]

MY FATHER HAD A MASSIVE STROKE *and I had to make some difficult decisions. My AHA! experience came when I realized that my grief was blocking my thinking. My Lizard Brain wanted everything possible done to keep him alive but my Wizard Brain knew that my father was in his eighties, loathed hospitals, was too weak to have surgery, and would want hospice care, not surgery. I chose hospice. Its staff was wonderful and he died peacefully, within a few days. I am so grateful that I was able to use my Wizard Brain and recognize that doing "everything" was not the best answer.*

Wise Way #2: Building a Strong Constellation of Support

Good friends are like stars. You might not always see them, but you know they are always there.
— Unknown

The second Wise Way, Building a Strong Constellation of Support, shows you a simple technique that will help you identify the people or sources to go to when you want to solve problems. At the same time, this process will make you think about who (or what) does not give help when you are in need. As you become aware of the kinds of connections that create a strong constellation of support, you will begin to seek out and use the most helpful sources.

Family and friends often are the people we first go to for help. Phrases such as "we are family," and "we are the world," extend the concept to describe a broader constellation — those who give you support beyond your inner circle of family and friends. It is important to think of help in this expanded sense, but it is also important to recognize the individuals who *truly* help you, as well as identify those who may make your problems worse.

Knowing how, when, and from whom to seek help involves higher brain functions in the prefrontal cortex or Wizard Brain. Visualizing the people and resources around you as a constellation of stars helps you understand how complex it can be to identify the people or sources you can use to help you solve a problem. There are many hidden stars. Use your thinking skills to find them and discover how they can help you.

The following story illustrates how a constellation of support works.

Farmer Brown's Constellation of Support

One morning, as Farmer Brown surveyed rows and rows of recently planted seedlings, he saw that those in a nearby field had been uprooted. The sun was rising, and if the seedlings were not replanted soon, they would wither and die. He grabbed a shovel and began to replant the field. As he did so, he noticed more uprooted seedlings in another field.

He used his cell phone to call his son, who was up at the farmhouse. Farmer Brown told his son to make some phone calls and then hurry down to the field to help. Soon, Farmer Brown's son, brother, and three neighboring farmers joined him and started replanting the seedlings.

Farmer Brown's Constellation of Support now looks like this:

Farmer Brown's Constellation of Support

A single line: People who are SOMEWHAT helpful. (———)

A line with crosshatches: People who are NOT helpful. (—/////—)

A double line: People who are VERY helpful. (=====)

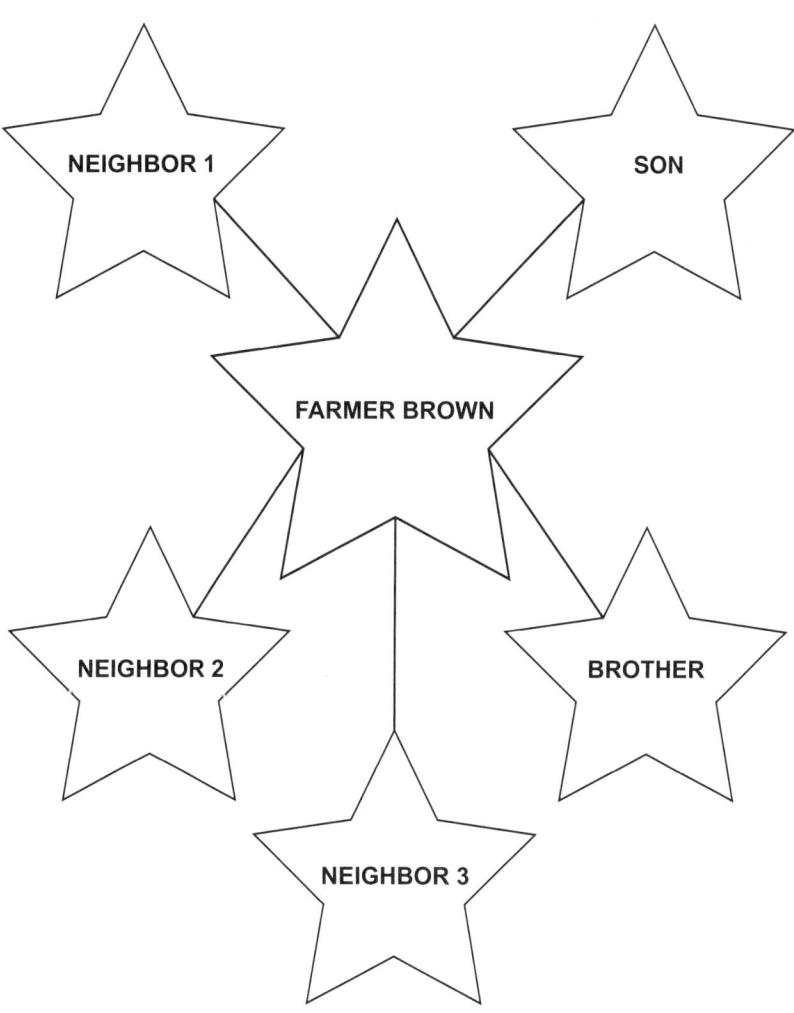

Farmer Brown and his helpers were almost finished replanting the seedlings when a passerby informed them that another field was uprooted. The three neighboring farmers could spare no more of their time and left.

Farmer Brown's brother stayed to help replant the other field, and he soon was finishing rows twice as quickly as Farmer Brown and his son. Taking a closer look, Farmer Brown saw that his brother's work was sloppy and ineffective. In his hurry, he was not planting the seedlings deep enough, and it was unlikely they would survive. When Farmer Brown mentioned this, his brother became very upset and stomped off in anger.

Farmer Brown's Constellation of Support now looks like this:

Farmer Brown's Constellation of Support

A single line: People who are SOMEWHAT helpful. (———)

A line with crosshatches: People who are NOT helpful. (—#####—)

A double line: People who are VERY helpful. (====)

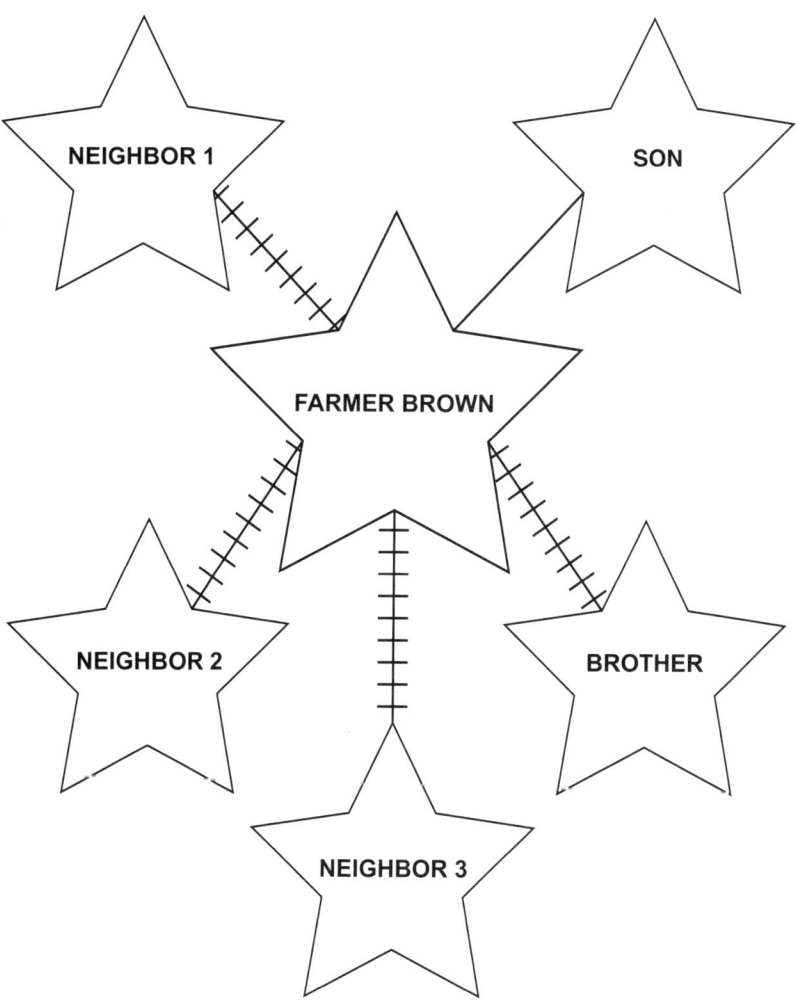

Farmer Brown and his son continued to work. The passerby reappeared and told them she had called the Agriculture Extension Office to ask for help and to see if anyone could determine the cause of the uprooted seedlings. She said the Extension Office contacted a crop expert from the agricultural college. The expert came over, found the cause of the problem, and solved it.

Farmer Brown's Constellation of Support

A single line: People who are SOMEWHAT helpful. (———)

A line with crosshatches: People who are NOT helpful. (–////–)

A double line: People who are VERY helpful. (====)

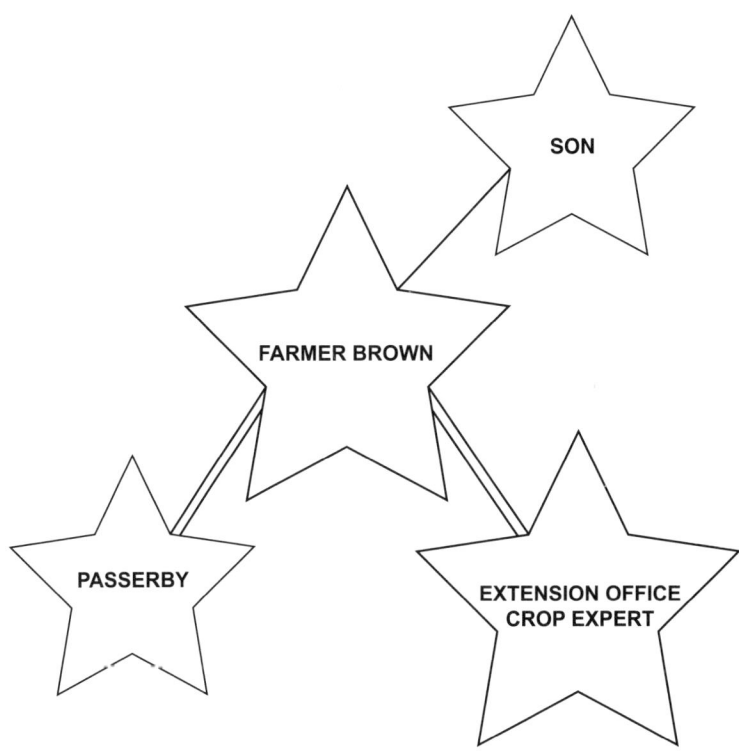

This story shows examples of Wizard Brain and Lizard Brain responses and illustrates the varied support people give as well as the changing nature of their support. People who use thinking skills can build strong Constellations of Support because they know how to:

(1) Identify the type of help needed to solve a problem.

(2) Go to the people or other resources that will be truly helpful in solving the problem.

(3) Evaluate the success of the problem-solving process.

(4) Make alternative plans if the problem is not improved or resolved.

Even if you cannot find the right person to help you, as a good thinker you will know how to use other resources for support. Reference books, help lines, search engines, and support groups are among the many available resources.

Using thinking skills means being able to recognize when family, close friends, or other sources of support are not helping you solve a problem. It also means being able to actively seek sources you never had considered and being aware that your support system changes from problem to problem.

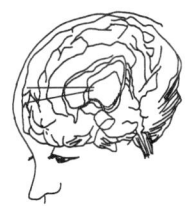

Build a Brain Connection

Practice this skill by doing the following:

• Observe how others use or don't use support systems. Think about who or what are the best sources of support. When you watch TV, read stories, or listen to the news, mentally identify the Constellations of Support for different characters.

• Make note of your behaviors and the behaviors of others that demonstrate Wizard Brain thinking or Lizard Brain reacting. Tie the behaviors in with the presence or absence of a strong Constellation of Support.

• Think about the changing nature of some sources of support and the static nature of others. Begin to think about sources of help you can use, and file them away for future reference.

• Think about a problem you have had. Who or what helped you solve the problem? Was the individual you thought would be helpful the best person? Did the type of support you received change during the process? What would you do differently next time?

AHA! Experience
[Shelly, divorcée with children]

AFTER MY DIVORCE, IT TOOK ME A LONG TIME to feel good about myself. I ran a business out of my home, and the only people I saw were my kids. I decided to join a health club and started going to a noon class. The women in my class became my Constellation of Support. They were a lifeline for me during a difficult period of my life.

[John, youth counselor]

I LEARNED THAT MY CONSTELLATION OF SUPPORT doesn't have to be a person. I have found great solace in reading scripture or other inspiring stories.

[Manuel, insurance agent]

LEARNING ABOUT THE CONSTELLATION OF SUPPORT made me realize that the people I thought would help me did not want me to succeed. I don't think that it was deliberate, but my own family did things to make sure that no one was "better" than anyone else.

Looking back, I realize that my family was more comfortable around failure than they were success. No one went to college. School was not an important accomplishment. I think realizing this was an AHA! moment.

I learned to get help from others. I talked with friends who were in college and found out who I should talk to. I called our community college and met with a counselor. She told me about a financial aid program and helped me apply for a scholarship and work/study position.

My family looked down on me and offered no encouragement. Many still make cutting remarks about my degree and job — but not everyone. My sister wants me to talk with her kids about school. I look for other young people who need encouragement to break the mold and do well in school. I want to be the person in their Constellation of Support who will help them succeed.

Wise Way #3:
Recognizing Red Flags

I am always ready to learn although I do not
always like being taught.
— Winston Churchill

The red flag is widely recognized as a symbol that warns of a dangerous situation. In BrainWise, the term Red Flag identifies internal and external signals that warn you that your Lizard Brain is beginning to activate itself. Learning to recognize Red Flags helps you use Wizard Brain thinking.

The Red Flags

Susan is helping her sister, Tara, purchase a new computer. They go to a big office warehouse that has advertised several models at very competitive prices.

The women are surprised they do not see any salespeople in the computer section. Eventually, Susan spots an employee at the end of an aisle and they walk toward his desk. He sees them but looks down and continues working on some papers. The women stand beside his desk, waiting for him to finish. The phone rings and he answers it without looking at the women.

He continues to ignore the women, turning his back as he talks on the phone. Susan is outraged. She feels her stomach turn and her muscles tighten. She clenches her teeth. Tara feels hot and her face turns red.

"I can't believe he didn't see us!" she whispers loudly to Susan. "He is waiting on the phone customer before us!"

Susan's mouth is dry and her heart beats fast. Her eyes pierce the back of the clerk.

"You're right. Let's get out of here. There are other stores that want our money."

The sisters stomp out of the store.

Susan and Tara exhibited a great many Red Flags during this incident.

Internal Red Flags are those you feel inside. Susan felt her stomach tighten, and Tara felt she was getting hot. Other signals include a rapid heartbeat, stomach turning, tight muscles, a dry mouth, a catch in your throat, and any number of sometimes subtle, sometimes severe, feelings inside your body.

Everyone has his or her own internal sensations that indicate something is not right. Recognizing and paying attention to those sensations helps you realize that you need to get your Wizard Brain involved.

External Red Flags are what you see, hear, or do. If the clerk had been observant, he would have noticed the sisters' drawn lips, red faces, and whispered comments. External Red Flags also include clenched fists, gritted teeth, a slammed door, shouting, or anything else that sends an auditory or visual warning. Still other external Red Flags can be facial expressions, unusual behavior, and unexplained changes in daily patterns.

People with good thinking skills pay attention to Red Flags. They are alert to cues and use them to assess and analyze a situation. Their brains pick up signals missed by people, like the clerk, who have not learned how to pay attention to and heed Red Flags.

With practice, you can recognize Red Flags automatically and use such information to ward off or prepare for problems. You also will understand what is meant when people say they "had a feeling" something was about to happen. They have learned to recognize certain Red Flags and know the importance of responding to them. Red Flags alert people to stop and think.

Individuals who are unaware of Red Flags or have not learned how to interpret them do not have this connection to their Wizard Brain. Without this hookup, they fall back on the Lizard Brain's impulse to react without thinking, just as was shown by the clerk's rude treatment of customers and the sisters' anger.

Red Flag warnings are an important part of the thinking process we use to assess and address problems. When you recognize Red Flags, you give your brain additional information to make decisions and create new pathways to your Wizard Brain.

As you learn additional thinking skills, you will see how they build on each other, adding more interference to the brain's tendency to react with Lizard Brain responses.

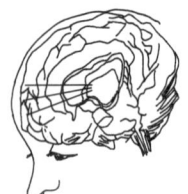

Build a Brain Connection

Practice recognizing Red Flags and the other thinking skills. Here are some suggested activities:

• Reread the story about Susan and Tara, identifying the various Red Flags throughout.

• In your own life, start to identify your internal Red Flags that signal a problem is imminent. In certain situations, do you find yourself becoming sweaty? Tense? Short of breath? Learn to heed your individual Red Flags as signs to proceed with caution.

• Be aware of your internal, gut-level feelings, and connect them with the external Red Flags you see, hear, taste, smell, and feel. Assess how you use these cues, and notice how your increasing awareness of this process prepares and improves your responses.

When people pick up external warnings or Red Flags, their bodies also react internally. For example, Cara always gets a tingling feeling when she feels something is not right. Now she uses that feeling to warn her that something is going to happen, and thinks about how to avoid a problem situation. Others describe their internal feelings as butterflies in the stomach, a heaviness in the heart or gut, twitching muscles, or feelings of tightness or warmth. Jake, a fireman, credits his sense of Red Flags with helping him anticipate a floor collapsing or a burst of flames exploding. "People think I have a premonition, but it is recognizing the Red Flags and acting on the warnings before anyone gets hurt."

• Mentally note the Red Flags you and others raise to warn of problems. Using this information along with your knowledge of the Wizard Brain/Lizard Brain and Constellation of Support will help you better analyze various problem situations.

AHA! Experience

[Mark, government employee]

IT IS TOO BAD THAT PEOPLE DON'T RECOGNIZE Red Flags until it is too late. How many times do we hear about tragedies because warnings went unheeded? I read that when the tsunami came after an earthquake on the ocean floor, the island people recognized a Red Flag: animals climbing to higher grounds. The island people who followed them were saved. They not only learned how to recognize Red Flags but also acted on them. I think that I am becoming pretty good at doing this. When I have a feeling that something is not right, a spot low in my heart feels different, almost like it is heavier. For me, this is a Red Flag that tells me to pay close attention to what is going on.

[Judy, kindergarten teacher]

I AM AN IDENTICAL TWIN, but my sister and I have very different personalities. She lives on the East Coast and I live on the West Coast. She went to an Ivy League college and I went to a state university. She's a high-level corporate executive and I'm a kindergarten teacher. We would always fight, and months would go by before we would speak to each other. Our fights became a family joke, but we found them too hurtful to be funny.

I have spent years trying to figure out why we do not get along. I was a psychology major and have sought answers in therapy, counseling, and numerous self-help approaches. Everything was temporary. Nothing worked until I used skills I learned in BrainWise.

*My AHA! moment came after I started teaching BrainWise to my kindergarten students. One day, I suddenly understood the trigger that caused my fights with my sister. It wasn't **what** she said to me, it was **the way she said it** that pushed my button and caused my Lizard Brain reactions. Her tone of voice was a Red Flag. Without fail, it would set me off.*

I made a conscious effort to pay attention to her voice and my gut-level feelings. It was amazing! For the first time in thirty years we could carry on a conversation and not fight because I had become aware of how such a stupid thing would trigger a fight. We now have long phone conversations and get along at family events. Our daughters are a few months apart and now they will have an opportunity to become friends, because their mothers are friends.

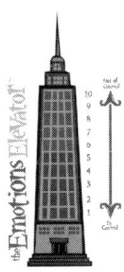

Wise Way #4:
Exiting the Emotions
Elevator

We all do no end of feeling and mistake it for thinking.
— Mark Twain

Twain's observation is as true today as it was 100 years ago. Mistaking feeling for thinking has serious consequences. "No end of feeling" can cause problems ranging from loss of friends to serious illness, and from failed marriages to toppled governments.

Unmanaged feelings result in anger, sadness, frustration, hatred, revenge, and irrational actions that underlie stress, depression, poor relationships, suicide, and violence. Feelings can make little problems seem big and big problems seem insurmountable. Being aware of how and why feelings overpower thinking helps you better control the "no end of feeling."

Emotions are an indispensable part of who we are. Although they underlie many problems, they also make us feel good. Learning how to control your emotions wisely is what Wise Way #4, Exiting the Emotions Elevator, is all about. It gives you thinking skills to manage your emotions.

This is important because emotional impulses also take a toll on your body. The following activity shows you how.

Make a fist and tightly squeeze and release it 120 times.

Did you get tired? Did your muscles feel tight?

This is how many times your heart beats per minute when your emotions are high. What kind of stress do you think this puts on the rest of your body? When your heart is beating overtime, the pace of your breathing increases, your muscles tighten, and you feel hot, restless, and agitated.

Think of your emotions as an elevator in a ten-story building. Intense, out-of-control emotions are on the top floors, and calm, easy-to-control emotions are on the lower floors. Your emotions can shoot to the tenth floor like a rocket, or they can inch up, floor by floor. The result is the same: When your emotions reach the top floor, you blow without thinking. Your Lizard Brain is engaged on the top floors and creates problems for you and others.

We don't feel a single emotion at a time but experience many feelings at once. It is important to recognize all your feelings and where they are relative to the ten floors. Red Flags already have tipped you off that your body is preparing to respond to a problem. Your job is to manage your emotions and keep them at a level where you can use your thinking skills. This is using your Wizard Brain.

People who seem to have fewer problems are able to stay off the Emotions Elevator or at least to remain on lower floors, where they can control their feelings. Knowing how to maintain control is another learned behavior.

Learning how to exit your Emotions Elevator will help you control your feelings. With practice, the following methods will help you get off of the Emotions Elevator or descend to a lower floor.

1. **Use "self-talk."** Tell yourself to calm down. Say things like "Easy, now." "It's not worth the trouble." "Don't get so upset." "Be careful." "Don't do anything stupid." Tell yourself you can handle the problem, you are in control, you have thinking skills, you know how to use your Wizard Brain — say whatever will help you get out of a volatile situation and let you stop and think!

2. **Tell yourself to *stop!*** Stop talking, stop fuming, stop eating — just tell yourself to stop! Get a grip and compose yourself so you can lower your emotions and handle the situation calmly and wisely.

3. **Leave the situation.** Give yourself a "time-out." Get away and calm down. If the problem persists, deal with it when you are off of the Emotions Elevator or on lower floors.

4. **Do something else.** This goes hand in hand with leaving the situation. Wash the car. Listen to music. Watch a movie. Call a friend. Read. Take a walk. Hit a punching bag. Do whatever it takes to distract yourself and redirect your emotions so you can Exit

your Emotions Elevator. Go back and deal with the problem when you are calm.

5. **Take deep breaths.** Count backward from ten and imagine that the elevator is going down one floor with each breath you take. Slowly breathe in through your nose and out through your mouth.

A good rule of thumb to remember is ***always stay lower on the Emotions Elevator than the other person!***

As you learn and practice methods to Exit your Emotions Elevator, you are building strong connections to your Wizard Brain. You also are creating banks of information for your brain to retrieve when you are faced with a problem. Instead of reacting, your brain will sort through all the information it has stored as memory, helping you to stop, think, and analyze a problem before you react. With use, the neural pathways you are building become stronger, solidifying connections with your other thinking skills and bypassing Lizard Brain reactions.

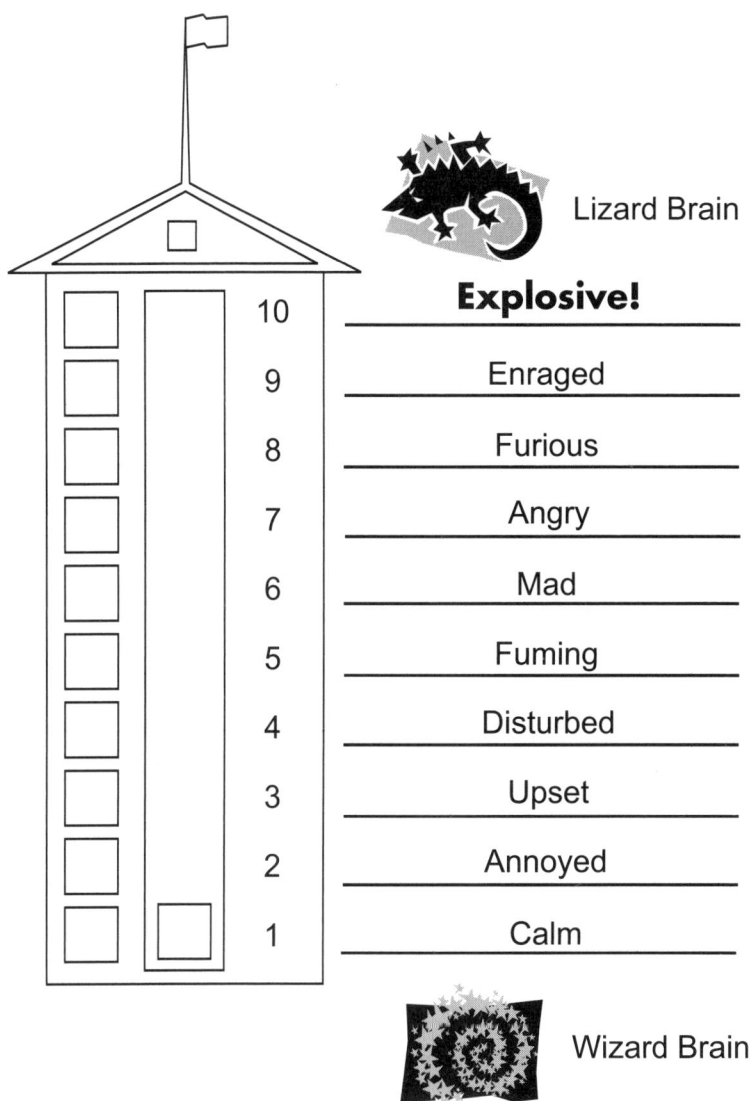

Lizard Brain

Explosive!

10	
9	Enraged
8	Furious
7	Angry
6	Mad
5	Fuming
4	Disturbed
3	Upset
2	Annoyed
1	Calm

Wizard Brain

Always be lower on the Emotions Elevator than the other person!

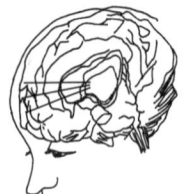

Build a Brain Connection

- To gain practice, integrate the concept of the Emotions Elevator into your assessment of everyday situations and activities. Ask yourself, "What floor of the Emotions Elevator is he or she on?" "What part of the brain is being used?" Judge whether he or she is demonstrating thinking skills. Evaluate your own responses, as well.

- Think about the resources you and others have used to deal with problems. Who or what resources were the most helpful? What Red Flags warned that a problem was imminent? Were emotions involved? Which ones? Where were they on the Emotions Elevator? What would help you get to a lower floor?

- Begin to use the BrainWise language and apply your new thinking skills daily. Mentally make note of situations demonstrating Wizard Brain thinking, Lizard Brain reactions, Constellations of Support, internal and external Red Flags, and the Emotions Elevator. Practice applying the concepts to yourself and others. With practice, you will find yourself automatically using thinking skills to examine problems.

AHA! Experience
[Wendy, teacher]

I AM A TEACHER, and the hand-squeezing exercise makes me think about not only what is going on inside me when I don't let go of problems, but what is going on inside the bodies of some of my students.

I attended a conference last year headlined by Dr. Bruce Perry, a national expert on traumatized children. I learned that the resting heart rate of an adult is 60–80 beats per minute and that a child's is 90–100 beats. Dr. Perry found that a traumatized child's resting heart rate, even after the child has been removed from the abusive situation, can be 120–160 beats per minute.

Their survival instinct clicks in and puts them in a state of constant vigilance, always on the alert and fearful of what will happen. The Emotions Elevator helps me understand and explain a very important concept to my students. Some anxiety is good, but it also is important to be aware of what stress can do to us and to know what we can do to stay off the Emotions Elevator or to descend to lower floors.

Wise Way #5: Separating Fact From Opinion

What people say, what people do, and what they say they do
are entirely different things.
— Margaret Mead

Confusing opinion with fact is the source of many problems. Emotions and the Lizard Brain's tendency to act irrationally fuel the untruths that perpetuate hurt feelings, hate, prejudice — even war.

You may remember the story of Chicken Little. An acorn falls on Chicken Little's head, and she thinks it means that the sky is falling. She convinces other animals to join her to "run and tell the king." On their way to the king, the last stop the worried group makes is at the house of a fox. He invites them in and eats them.

Chicken Little, and the unfortunate animals she convinced, mixed up fact and opinion. Their emotions caused them to act without thinking, erasing the Red Flags that could have warned them that the fox was dangerous. The fox took advantage of their Lizard Brain reaction.

Gossip and false information underlie many problems. Opinions mixed with emotions are a dangerous combination that can lock people into Lizard Brain reactions, just like Chicken Little.

Opinions play a big part in the following story.

Full of Opinions

Kirk and Joline Smith and their teenagers, Sam and Dea, were listening to a radio talk show. The discussion was about a well-known celebrity who had been accused of being a sexual predator. The family listened with interest to comments by the talk show host and the people who called in. Kirk and Sam took different positions than Joline and Dea.

"I can't stand him! I hope he gets what's coming to him," said Dea.

Her mother agreed. "Men who are predators like that need to be locked up!"

"The woman dropped the charges," said Kirk.

"That means nothing. She was probably pressured to do that. He has lots of money and high-paid lawyers. They used their power and money to shut her up," Dea retorted.

"We don't know what happened," said Kirk. "We only know what we read in the newspaper. How do you know the accusations are true?"

"She couldn't have made something like that up! It sounds just like the kind of thing a man like him would do," said Joline.

Sam protested, "Oh, Mom. Girls make things up all the time!"

Kirk interrupted. "You are all going overboard and expressing opinions. Sam, girls do not make things up 'all the time.' Dea, just because someone has money does not mean that they can buy their way out of everything. And Joline, I agree that people who are guilty of being a sexual predator should be locked up, but he is innocent until proven guilty. In this case, we will never know because the charges have been dropped."

"Well, I'm not the only one who is outraged!" Joline said.

"Yeah!" Dea agreed.

"Yes, a lot of people are emotionally involved in this case," Kirk acknowledged. "But this kind of situation requires that you step away from your emotions. We don't know the facts. We are getting our information from the media and from talk show hosts. What kind of interest do they have in stirring up controversy?"

"It will give them higher ratings," said Sam.

"That could be. My point is to not be so quick to jump to conclusions, especially when you do not know if the information is true," his dad replied.

Good thinkers know the difference between fact and opinion and use this knowledge to make wise decisions. A fact is something that can be proven to be true. An opinion is something you think is true, but for which you have no proof. What are the facts in the previous story? What are opinions?

A good way to demonstrate the difference between fact and opinion is to look at a picture and describe what you see. The following picture of Denver International Airport shows you an example.

Photo courtesy of DIA

FACTS

- Its roof is made of heavy duty teflon material.

- The roof design is a series of shapes that look like cones.

- You can see light shining through the canvas.

- A curving road runs in front of the structure.

- There are clouds in the sky.

- It is a picture of Denver International Airport.

OPINIONS

- The circus has come to town.

- It is the most efficient and best designed airport in the world.

- The roof will collapse when it snows.

- It will cost a fortune in upkeep.

- They built it too far from the city.

- People will judge Denver by its airport.

It is easy to have opinions and make assumptions, especially when they are grounded in emotions. Wise people use their thinking skills to analyze the information their senses gather and send to the brain. When separating fact from opinion — whether dealing with gossip or reports of weapons of mass destruction — we must learn how to overcome our emotions and the Lizard Brain instinct that causes us to react impulsively.

You can see how being aware of the thinking process helps you understand your behavior and that of others. Even young children can learn this concept. After the Columbine High School shootings in Colorado, a kindergarten teacher reported that her students were able to discuss the difficult events in terms of the 10 Wise Ways. The children said the killers were using their Lizard Brains because they were on the tenth floor of their Emotions Elevators. They identified "hate," "anger," "getting even," "being mad," and "sadness" as emotions underlying the violent behavior.

When one of the students said that someone might do the same thing at their school, the class decided that was an opinion, not a fact. The children separated facts from opinions and made a list of facts that showed why a similar incident would not happen at their school. Recognizing the connection between Lizard Brain thinking, the constellation of support, red flag warnings, and the emotions elevator promotes Wizard Brain thinking to separate fact from opinions. This thinking process defuses potentially volatile situations and decreases problems.

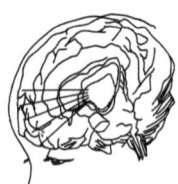

Build a Brain Connection

- To practice using this skill, become aware of the facts and opinions in situations that involve you and those around you. Mentally question the accuracy of statements. If possible, respectfully challenge questionable statements. Ask, "Is that a fact or an opinion?"

- Be aware that Lizard Brain users will claim their opinions are facts, and they may not have the skills to recognize their faulty thinking. Be careful and always assess where the person you are challenging is on his or her Emotions Elevator. Look for Red Flags that signal potential problems.

- As you begin to use and link the Wise Ways, you are strengthening the neural connections to your Wizard Brain. The powerful Lizard Brain's emotions and impulsive actions still may override the connections you are building, but you now are aware of what's happening — not only to yourself, but to others.

AHA! Experience

[Tom, army private]

I LISTEN TO TALK RADIO SHOWS AND READ INTERNET BLOGS. Wow! Opinions are gossip and they are a big industry! It is hard to remove your emotions from issues, but I am learning to recognize that emotions cause a lot of my problems. When I am lower on the Emotions Elevator, I am able to think about facts and opinions and to decide if something is really true. I never did that before. It is amazing how such a little thing has made my life better! I see other people getting all bent out of shape over something they think is true, and in my head I automatically ask, "Fact or opinion?" I can't believe how much of my life used to be driven by opinions.

[Laura, battered woman]

FACT VERSUS FICTION REALLY HIT HOME when I finally understood what everyone had been trying to tell me. I was in love with J.R. and thought he was everything I wanted. And he was, but only when we first started dating. I am sure that selective memory helped me deny how much he changed. After a few months, he didn't want me to see my friends or family. He told me that if I loved him, I would spend all my time with him. When my friends warned me that he was too controlling, he told me that they were just jealous and spreading gossip. My mother and sister also raised questions, but I ignored them, too. I thought they didn't want to see me happy.

After we had dated for a while, J.R. would get mad at me over things like wearing the wrong blouse or preparing food he didn't like. Soon the little fights grew into bigger fights and he started hurting me by twisting my arms, pinning me down, and grabbing my hair. Then he started hitting me.

He was extremely sorry after these episodes, and I would forgive him. I hid my bruises with makeup and long sleeves and believed that he meant what he said. I accepted as fact his promises that he would never hurt me again — I never questioned that what he was saying was not true. My AHA! experience was realizing the fact that he was a batterer.

I had wanted so badly to believe him that I was blind to all the Red Flags telling me to get out. I treated the advice of others as jealous gossip and false comments. I realized that nothing was going to change, no matter how much I wanted to believe it. With support from my family, I left the relationship. It was one of the best things I have done.

Wise Way #6: Asking Questions and Gathering Information

You can tell whether a man is clever by his answers.
You can tell whether a man is wise by his questions.
— Naguib Mahfouz

We ask questions in all kinds of situations. But learning how to ask the right questions involves using thinking skills. Stopping to think helps us better assess a problem and determine what further information we need to make good decisions. The following story illustrates this point.

The professor gave his class a problem. On a chart in front of the room he wrote, "She turned, looked at him, and ran."

He said, "I want you to figure out what happened by asking me questions. I will answer all your questions, but I want you to know that one question will give you the answer. Try to figure out what question will give you the answer."

Students began raising their hands and he started calling on them.

"Where did this happen?" asked the first student. The professor wrote the question underneath the statement.

"At a house," replied the professor, and he called on another student.

"Where in the house?" asked the second student. The professor wrote this question under the first one.

"In the bedroom," said the professor. He called on another student.

"Why did she run?" asked the third student. As he wrote down her question, he replied, "Because she was scared."

The next question asked was, "Why was she scared?" The professor wrote it underneath the others. He said, "She thought he was going to hurt her."

"How old was he?" asked the next student. The professor listed this question under the others.

"He was thirty years old," the professor responded.

"How old was she?" was the next query.

"She was eight," the professor replied as he wrote the question down.

The class was buzzing after this answer. They still had not asked the right question, but the answers they had received painted an unpleasant situation.

"You have asked six questions but not the right one. I will take two more questions," the professor told the class.

"Why were they at the house?" asked another student.

"Because they lived there," said the professor. He wrote the question down and said, "One more question."

"Were they related?" asked a student.

"No," said the professor. He wrote the question on the chart.

He read the questions back to the class. "Where did this happen?" "Where in the house?" "Why did she run?" "Why was she scared?"

"How old was he?" "How old was she?" "Why were they at the house?" "Were they related?"

"These are good questions," he said. "Often, when we need information, we don't ask the right questions, and we form opinions from partial information. This causes problems."

The class waited. "I think this exercise gives you a good example of how this can happen." He paused. "'Who is she?' is the question that answers the riddle. And the answer is, 'a cat.'"

The class broke into a relieved titter. The professor smiled. "It happens every time," he said.

Learning to ask the right questions takes time. With practice, you will discover that your brain is able to quickly retrieve information you have stored and rapidly sort through the knowledge you have fed it, selecting what you need to ask the right questions. If you have not learned or practiced thinking skills, your brain resorts to Lizard Brain reactions.

You already have learned to ask some important questions related to the 10 Wise Ways:

- Is my or someone else's behavior based on Wizard Brain thinking or Lizard Brain reacting?

- What resources are available for support? To whom can I go for help? What services can I use?

- What Red Flags signal a problem?

- What emotions are being felt and on what floor of the Emotions Elevator are they? What can be done to go to a lower floor or get off the elevator?

- Is the underlying issue a fact or an opinion? How can the fact be proven?

- What questions will help me get the information I need to make a good decision?

Consistently asking these questions — and collecting and using information to analyze problems — builds the thinking process in your brain, giving your brain more material to make wise decisions. Instead of reacting, your brain bypasses the Lizard Brain and links up with the increasingly busy pathways connecting to your Wizard Brain, which helps you retrieve information to make good choices and solve problems.

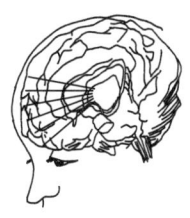

Build a Brain Connection

- To practice Wise Way #6, ask questions that integrate the Wise Ways into everyday problems. Take into account the Wizard and Lizard Brains, the Constellation of Support, Red Flags, the Emotions Elevator, and Fact Versus Opinion.

  Ask yourself, "What would be the best question to ask to help me get the answer(s) I need to solve this problem?"

- Continue to assess situations using all the Wise Ways. This process takes time only during the initial learning phase. As you internalize the skills, analyzing problems will become an automatic part of your response.

All the skills you are learning in BrainWise build on and relate to each other. Asking questions related to the 10 Wise Ways is an important component of this structure.

AHA! Experience
[Derrick, computer analyst]

IT ISN'T AS EASY AS IT SEEMS TO LEARN how to ask the right questions. Looking back, I see that it does involve using all the other wise ways, because you have to size up each situation and figure out what information you need. This whole process hit home when I was picked to serve on a jury.

The case involved a man charged with stalking his former girlfriend. I always thought some things were pretty clear-cut, but I learned that "without a doubt" can be a heavy burden.

The jury was evenly divided after the evidence was presented. Some jurors thought the woman was overreacting and trying to get even, but others believed she had good reasons to be afraid of the accused. I was voted jury foreman and empathized with both sides.

It's amazing how you form opinions about people because of the way they look, dress, and talk. The accused was well dressed and nice-looking. I thought the woman looked mousy and found myself thinking she was charging him to ruin his reputation after he had dumped her. The attorneys did a good job because I found myself going back and forth supporting one, then the other.

The trial ended with good arguments made by both sides. In the jury room, I posed one question: What are the facts? By focusing on this central question and avoiding the courtroom theatrics and emotional arguments, we were able to dissect and discuss the evidence, carefully separating facts from opinions. We compiled information that helped us make an informed decision. It was difficult to discount the emotions and Lizard Brain reactions, but we did. In the end, we found the accused guilty.

After the trial, we found out that he had told a coworker that he would get even with his girlfriend for leaving him. He had not dumped her; she really had dumped him! I was glad that we had not let our opinions about unattractive women and good-looking men cloud our judgment. We had asked the right kinds of questions we needed to get information to make a good decision.

Wise Way #7:
IDentifying Your Choices
(IDC)

We can try to avoid making choices by doing nothing,
but even that is a decision.
— Gary Collins

People who tend to rely on their Lizard Brain often act as if they have only one option, whereas people with thinking skills realize they have many choices. This is one of the differences separating people with more problems from people with fewer problems.

The following illustrates how to use Wise Way #7, IDentifying Your Choices (IDC).

You arrive at the movie theater early to save seats for yourself and two friends. The movie has received good reviews and the theater is filling up.

Two people head toward the seats you have saved and you politely tell them, "These seats are taken." The man glares at you and says, "Screw you! We're sitting here!" He and his companion take the seats.

What is the first thought that goes through your mind? Situations like this can elicit intense emotions that rocket you up the Emotions Elevator. Lizard Brain reactions — from mumbled curses to a fistfight — are all too common.

Other options in this situation include to do nothing and sit in shocked or angry silence, talk with the theater manager, wait for your friends, or move to other seats.

IDentifying Your Choices, or IDC, teaches you to consider the many options available in a situation. It is important to remember that making no choice is a choice in itself. By learning to identify all your choices, you send signals to your Wizard Brain for analysis, and it uses the banks of information it has stored. You already know that the more information the brain has gathered and can access, the more neural pathways are available for your brain to make problem-solving connections.

BrainWise gives you words to understand and describe what is going on, creating a structure your brain can use to process problems.

Let's return to the problem with the theater seats. Because of your thinking skills, you realize that:

- The people who took the saved seats are using their Lizard Brains.

- The man's threatening tone and posture are Red Flags signaling trouble. You also may experience and recognize your own internal Red Flags, such as a rapid heartbeat or flushed sensation.

- You at first were annoyed but became more upset by the way the man and his companion defied you. You recognize that you are going up the Emotions Elevator. You feel angry, insulted, surprised, and threatened. You realize you may do something stupid if you don't calm down. You sense that the man who took the seats is a bully and a powder keg of emotions, ready to explode.

- You must lower your position on the Emotions Elevator using control self-talk. You tell yourself to calm down, that this situation could get out of control very quickly. You continue to use self-talk:

  – Even though it is a fact that you arrived early to save seats for your friends, no theater rule says those seats are yours.

  – You ask yourself, "What is the best way to handle this?"

- You do an IDC (Identifying Your Choices):

  – You can create a scene.

  – You can sit and let your anger build and create a big scene with your friends when they arrive.

  – You can do nothing — your friends are late and they will have to find other seats.

  – You can wait for your friends and ask them what they want to do.

  – You can flag down an employee and ask him to get the manager.

  – You can move and save seats elsewhere.

Lizard Brain users act on their emotions, which creates a volatile situation in this scenario! When you are not able to stop and think, you react. But by using your thinking skills, you will find yourself rapidly analyzing problem situations such as this one.

The more you engage in the thinking process, the greater your ability becomes to use thinking skills to address problems. You are laying the groundwork for making connections among all 10 Wise Ways. With practice, your brain will be able to process all of these steps at warp speed, picking and choosing the skills for each problem situation.

IDentifying Your Choices, or IDC, helps expand your perception of problems. Recognizing that you always have choices — and that not making a choice is also a choice — is an important part of the thinking process. IDC prepares you for Wise Way #8: Considering the Consequences of your choices.

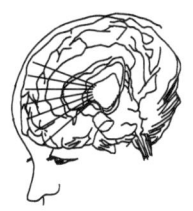 **Build a Brain Connection**

The following activities will give you practice IDentifying your Choices (IDC).

- Examine the choices you and others make in different situations. Assess whether thinking or emotions and impulse spurred the choice.

- Become aware of the interplay among poor choices, Lizard Brain responses, a faulty or nonexistent Constellation of Support, Red Flags, elevated emotions, mistaking opinions for fact, and not asking questions or gathering information.

- Practice recognizing the presence or absence of thinking skills in problem situations, and identify how that influenced the choices that were made.

AHA! Experience
[Maria, hotel employee]

I NEVER USED TO THINK ABOUT CHOICES because I always used my Lizard Brain. I laid blame on everyone else. Nothing was my fault. My unhappiness was because of bad luck, bad genes, or was someone else's fault. Life was unfair and I was its victim.

I had learned about BrainWise and the wise ways at a job training class. At first, I thought it was stupid and was just another course I was forced to take. But something strange happened.

One day, my car would not start. I was mad and was ready to blow off the day instead of going to work. For some reason, I found myself remembering IDC and that I always had other choices. I thought about what else I could do and came up with some interesting options.

I could take the bus, but I'd have to find out the schedule and get the right change. I could call my sister and see if she could give me a ride, but she was probably gone by now. I could call a taxi, but I didn't want to spend the money. I could call work and see if someone could come get me, but that would be an awkward call to make. My next-door neighbor had a couple of bikes, and I jokingly thought I could borrow a bike from her.

But the more I thought about it, the more appealing the idea of riding a bike to work became.

I don't know why. Maybe it was because it was such a nice day. Maybe I was fantasizing about Lance Armstrong. Maybe I was remembering the fun I had riding my bike as a kid. Anyway, I went next door and my very surprised neighbor kindly lent me a bike.

I still can't believe I did it. I got on and started pedaling. I was sure that I looked like the Wicked Witch of the West, but that thought made me laugh and pedal faster. I imagined I was in Kansas and outrunning a tornado. In no time at all, I was at work.

To make a long story short, I bought my own bike and started riding it not only to work, but everywhere else. I lost weight, made new friends, and felt great. One of the most amazing things was that the migraine headaches I had suffered for years decreased and then went away. It was a miracle! Riding that bike was one of the best choices I ever made.

Consequences
(CNL) (CAO)

Wise Way #8: Considering Consequences

How much more grievous are the consequences of anger
than the causes of it?
— Marcus Aurelius

Some of us never have learned, or may have forgotten, an important lesson: With every privilege comes a responsibility. Understanding and accepting responsibility requires that we consider the consequences of our choices. BrainWise teaches two ways to examine choices: First, we consider the Consequences Now and Later (CNL); and second, we consider the Consequences Affecting Others (CAO).

Wizard Brain users not only recognize they have more than one choice, they assess their choices by weighing the consequences. To do so, we need to be off the Emotions Elevator or on one of the lower floors. When we lower our emotions, the brain is able to access the information needed for analysis.

With Wise Way #8, you are building additional pathways to your Wizard Brain. Your brain seeks answers to the questions you are learning to ask about choices: "If I make this choice, what is the consequence now?" "What would be the consequence later?" "What is the consequence affecting others?"

This process often incorporates other thinking skills as the brain sorts through related experiences and assembles information you can use to consider consequences. "Do I need help?" "To whom, or what, should I turn for the most useful help or information?" "Do I need time to think about this?" "What are the facts of this situation?" "Why am I uncomfortable making this choice?" "What did I learn from previous similar situations?" "What will happen if I make this choice?" "What will happen if I don't?"

The brain, however, does much more than ask crucial questions. The neural pathways you are building with thinking skills overturn your instinct to act emotionally and impulsively. Your brain now has other routes it can take to process a problem. In a flash, these pathways access pertinent information, review memories, and retrieve answers. Thinking jump-starts your brain to search, assess, and analyze — overcoming its basic impulse to react.

As you start to access all your thinking skills — reviewing choices and their consequences — you begin to recognize that many people lack these skills. This realization can help you understand their erratic, unthinking behavior.

Every problem presents different choices and consequences. As you practice thinking skills, your brain gleans information and files it in different memory banks. The brain remembers what happened when you

made good choices and what happened when
bad ones. People who have learned to use thin
are creating a web of neural connections in thei
Brain that can access relevant information and ᴜᴏᴄ it to
make decisions.

CNL involves thinking about the present and the future, and CAO involves thinking about other people — two processes involving complex reasoning. It is a learning process and takes time, but everyone has the ability to apply multiple thinking skills simultaneously. It's simply a matter of learning and practicing how to do so. Considering consequences — letting those logical beacons guide your decisions — is an important component of the thinking process. Without practice, however, IDC, CNL, and CAO often are omitted from the problem-solving process.

When you learn awareness of consequences, you are likely to recognize that this depth of thinking frequently is lacking in choices made by other people — even people in high positions. Recognizing the absence or presence of thinking skills in others is additional information for your brain to store and use when you are solving problems.

You can see how the thinking process is getting a bit more complicated. Not only are you learning to identify more choices, but now you are learning to consider the consequences — CNL as well as CAO — of each choice you have identified in a problem situation.

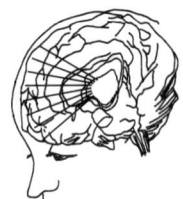

Build a Brain Connection

Wise Way #7 asked you to think about problems and identify several choices in response. Wise Way #8 takes this a step further and asks you to examine each choice by considering the Consequences Now and Later (CNL) as well as the Consequences Affecting Others (CAO).

- From now on, add CNL and CAO to your mental assessment of choices for problems — yours and others. Consider the CNL and CAO of historical and current events such as election outcomes, business transactions, education success or failure, wars, droughts, conservation, vaccines, media — anything and everything related to choices you or others have made.

  Ask yourself:

  "What is the consequence now of making, or not making, this choice? What will be the consequence later if I do, or do not, make this choice?"

  "If I do, or do not, make this choice, what effect will this choice have on others?"

- Continue to integrate the Wise Ways into everyday situations — your interactions with other people, current events, and decisions you make.

- Continue to mentally note the presence or absence of thinking skills in others, including their ability to consider the consequences of their actions.

With practice, you will find that your brain quickly sizes up a problem and applies CNL and CAO to all the thinking skills you have learned.

AHA! Experience
[Bob, banker]

THE BRAINWISE PROGRAM SAVED MY LIFE. Things were pretty bad and I felt like I wanted to end it all. I felt so bad and hopeless that I was even thinking about how I was going to kill myself. Somehow, in the middle of all my dark thoughts, different wise ways started popping up. Maybe making those brain connections paid off!

CAO (Consequences Affecting Others) came into my head first. I thought about the people I would hurt and how they would react. I knew I would hurt some people that I really cared about. I also thought about CNL (Consequences Now and Later). Ending my life would solve my problems, but afterwards, it would create problems for others. It might even push someone else to commit suicide.

I thought about my Constellation of Support. I was not good about telling people close to me about my dark thoughts. I knew people would want to help, but they weren't able to because I never shared this side of me with anyone. It made me start thinking that maybe I should ask someone for help.

I was feeling sad, hopeless, and angry to the point that I thought I would burst from the pain. I was overwhelmed and felt like a heavy rock was weighing my whole body down. I could hardly breathe. I started taking deep breaths and suddenly remembered to slowly breathe in through my nose and out through my mouth.

I started counting and imagining I was going down a floor on the Emotions Elevator with each breath.

At the same time, I used control self-talk and started telling myself that others have pulled themselves out of situations much worse than mine, and that I could, too.

Thinking about consequences was the first step that helped me get out of the darkness and despair that surrounded me. It took time to change my attitude and the way I felt, but nothing was ever as bad as it was at this time. The thinking skills I learned in BrainWise saved my life. I use them every day.

Wise Way #9: Setting Goals and Plans for Action

If you aim for nothing, you will hit it every time.
— Unknown

Every day we have goals — to be happy, be a top performer, lose weight, earn a degree, be a good parent, stop smoking, or anything else we want to achieve.

Attaining goals requires you to use all the wise ways and apply awareness of them not only to yourself, but to those with whom you interact. Wizard Brain users are successful at reaching goals because their brains have pathways connecting all their thinking skills, giving them access to the broad range of information they need to form a goal and a plan for achieving it.

To illustrate the importance of properly setting goals, a manager held a meeting of all her employees and presented the following exercise.

She handed every employee a sheet of paper and told them they must follow two rules: They could ask no questions, and they must keep their eyes closed.

She then gave the following instructions:

"Fold your paper in half." She waited as each employee hesitantly folded his or her paper.

"Now tear a piece off the end of the paper." The employees slowly felt the edges of their papers. Someone asked, "Which end?" The manager said, "No questions."

When several participants opened their eyes, she quickly said, "Remember to keep your eyes closed!"

She then directed her employees to unfold the paper and refold it in the other direction. When finished, they were instructed to "tear off another piece."

The room was quiet except for the sound of rustling papers and occasional mumblings of confusion from the group.

"We are almost finished," the manager said. "Next, fold one side of the paper and tear a hole in the center."

When everyone had complied, she said, "Now open your eyes and hold up your papers."

The employees opened their eyes, unfolded their papers, and looked around. Everyone's paper was different.

The manager said, "I gave everyone the same directions. Why do all the papers look different?"

The answers came quickly. "We didn't know how we were supposed to do it." "People interpreted the directions differently." "We couldn't see what we were doing." "We couldn't ask questions."

The manager said, "Yes, those are all good answers. If our goal was to have all of the papers look the same, what would you do differently?"

Now that they had a goal, the group identified strategies and formed a plan. They changed the rules, allowing participants to keep their eyes open and ask questions. They worked together, asking questions, identifying choices, and creating a plan that could be successfully implemented not only by their group, but by others.

Using a Constellation of Support, recognizing Red Flags, keeping low on the Emotions Elevator, separating facts from opinions, asking questions, identifying choices, considering consequences — all are involved in setting goals and forming plans for action.

As you become aware of and practice using more wise ways, you will better understand why people who never have learned them find it difficult to set and reach goals.

Remember, the strong urge to act on impulse sometimes wins out as the Lizard Brain takes over. People with thinking skills rebound quickly because they know they will learn from their mistakes.

Setting goals involves complex reasoning — the ability to simultaneously evaluate a problem and process potential solutions using multiple thinking skills. BrainWise makes you aware of this process and gives you tools to practice your thinking while setting realistic goals and formulating the plans necessary to achieve them.

Attaining goals requires you to use all the wise ways and apply them not only to yourself, but to those with whom you interact. Wizard Brain users are successful at reaching goals because their brains have pathways connecting all their thinking skills, giving them access to the broad range of information needed to form, work toward, and achieve goals.

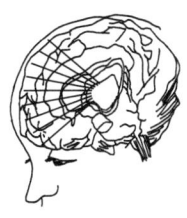

Build a Brain Connection

Every day we set and achieve goals. To prevent cavities, we brush our teeth. To get a good job, we get education and training. To be happy, we find out what it takes to make us satisfied and make sure it becomes part of our lives.

- Begin to look at life and problem situations in terms of the wise ways. As you think about problems, include a goal in your analysis. Ask yourself, "What is my goal and what is my plan to reach it?" The folding papers exercise showed you that having a stated goal makes it easier to plan for and achieve the outcome you want.

- Be aware of unrealistic goals you and others may have. It is easier to reach a goal of losing two pounds than thirty pounds. Learn to break goals down into actions that give you results and will help you reach your final goal.

- Practice setting goals with action plans you can achieve. If you need to see results quickly, set short-term goals and build up to long-term goals.

Setting goals requires using all the wise ways you have learned. You are building skills that will help you set goals and make plans to take action, affecting events that will influence not only you, but others.

AHA! Experience
[Jim, investment consultant]

IT'S STRANGE HOW YOU HEAR ABOUT SOMETHING *but it never really means anything to you, and suddenly you have an AHA! experience. I have heard about setting goals since I was a kid, but it had never sunk in. Now I know that you must do a lot of thinking to achieve your goals.*

I had been overweight for years, a problem compounded by my love of food and beer. Making matters worse was my twelve-year smoking habit.

Every New Year, articles and ads appear for diets, health clubs, and quit-smoking clinics. I knew all methods had a poor success rate. I was not heavy (or rich) enough to qualify for weight-loss surgery but knew that even this drastic method did not have long-term success. The percent of people with lasting weight loss is so small, researchers have created a national registry to study them!

I used these facts to justify my resistance to dieting. The funny thing is, knowing this information also made me be smart about how I approached my own diet when I was finally ready to make a change.

I don't know what the trigger was; it was probably a combination of things. I was tired of being tired. I was tired of being out of breath. I was worried about my blood pressure. I couldn't do things with my kids. I didn't like what I saw in the mirror. I knew that if I was serious about improving my health, I had to take responsibility and make major changes in my life.

My goal was to be healthier. To achieve this, I had to lose weight, stop smoking, and cut down on my drinking. I felt that I was ready to do it and was highly motivated to stick with a plan. I was determined to join that elite club of rare individuals who not only reach their diet and smoking goals, but also maintain them for the rest of their lives.

I knew I was dealing with some serious Lizard Brain reactions. Food and tobacco were automatic bad habits — my brain was programmed to reward me with food and cigarettes. I had to make a plan to switch to making wiser choices. My plan involved using every thinking skill I had learned. First, I acknowledged that my eating was pure Lizard Brain, based on emotions and impulses. Then, using other wise ways, I devised a plan I felt would work for me.

If you have ever prepared a room for painting, you know that 80 percent of the work is getting the walls ready to take the paint. In the same way, I did a lot of mental prepping and planning before I even started trying to make life changes.

I knew that certain people — friends who were smokers and overweight family members and friends — would sabotage my efforts. I would not tell them about my plans, even when pressured. I thought about ways I could refuse their offers without raising suspicion. For example, I would decline sugar-laced products, including alcohol, because sugar gives me a headache. With smoking and alcohol, I said I was cutting back because of medicine I was taking. It worked like a charm — no one questioned me!

I used all of the wise ways to develop strategies and form a success plan, including ways I could handle cravings and other battles I would face. I knew that having a goal and a plan was worthless if you don't use them, and I was determined to succeed!

It takes an incredible effort to beat the odds and to lose weight and quit smoking. I think I was mentally prepared to take the challenge. Believe me, that Lizard Brain is always pulling you back! But my thinking skills helped me keep my cravings and emotions low on the Emotions Elevator. So did knowing that I had choices and remembering the consequences of those choices.

Now I really understand what it means to have goals and develop plans for action. I can't imagine living any other way.

Wise Way #10: Communicating Effectively

The obvious is that which is never seen until someone expresses it simply.
— Kahlil Gibran

Communicating effectively — the last of the 10 Wise Ways — completes the set of thinking skills needed to make a lifetime of wise decisions. Good communication involves the simultaneous use of all the wise ways. Wizard Brain thinkers multitask when they communicate; Lizard Brain users react.

Communicating is a complex task. Breaking it down into three parts makes effective communication easier to learn and retain.

1. Nonverbal Communication

Body Messages. People who use thinking skills are aware of the messages sent by nonverbal behavior — theirs and others. They know these body messages can be Red Flags warning people of problems, but the messages also can be reassuring and positive. Good thinkers are able not only to display appropriate nonverbal messages themselves, but they are skilled at accurately interpreting body messages sent by others.

Do you want to be taken seriously? Think about the message you want to send and position yourself to deliver it. Establishing eye contact, facing the person directly, judging how close to stand to an individual, and making appropriate facial expressions and hand or arm gestures all are important facets of effective communication.

Appropriate body messages are powerful cues wise people use to communicate effectively.

2. Verbal Communication

Ideally, your words go hand in hand with your body messages. Many people are unaware that their body language is not consistent with what they are saying. The following techniques, coupled with corresponding body language, help send clear messages.

Avoiding Double Messages. Some people say one thing, but their voice and body language indicate they mean another. We have all heard the phrase "Your lips say 'no,' but your eyes say 'yes.'" Good communicators send consistent messages and are not betrayed by their body language. They also recognize the double messages sent by others and are able to assess whether those messages are deliberate or unintentional.

Every communication situation is different. It is important to recognize Red Flags, manage your emotions, and use your other thinking skills to analyze the messenger's intention.

Using "I" Messages. "I" messages are a very effective way to communicate without offending the other person. It takes considerable practice to become skilled in using "I" messages.

When you use "I" messages, you take responsibility for your feelings rather than attacking the other person. "You" statements, on the other hand, are threatening and blame the other. They push the buttons of other people's Emotions Elevators, sending them skyward. In Lizard Brain terms, they threaten the other person, who then reacts emotionally and impulsively.

Many occasions that require "I" messages involve intense emotions. "I" statements help to defuse volatile situations.

Compare the following examples of "you" statements and "I" statements:

"You never listen to me!"

"You always say that!"

"You have to get the last word in, don't you?"

"I want to be heard and feel like I am not."

"I have heard this before."

"I get upset in situations like this."

For practice, become aware of "I" messages and identify when they are used to communicate effectively. Observe how quickly you or others shoot up the Emotions Elevator when accusatory "you" statements are used, and note the difference when you use "I" statements.

Effective use of "I" statements also requires linking what you say to the other wise ways. This means using multiple thinking skills at once. If your Lizard Brain has dominated how you communicate, you will need to practice using "I" statements.

To become fluent in "I" statements, you must move lower on your Emotions Elevator so you can think about how to phrase your statement while, at the same time, considering its consequences. A good method is to practice using "I" messages in nonemotional situations. For example, when you are a detached observer watching someone else's problem on a television show or movie, or listening to a heated conversation on talk radio, assess the communication skills the participants are using.

In your mind, replace accusatory and inflammatory statements with "I" messages, and think about how they could be used to defuse the situations. Then, when your brain is familiar with the process, you will be more likely to access and use the technique when faced with a problem situation.

Recognize Differences Without Making Judgments. Lizard Brain users respond to differences as threats, which elicit intense feelings. Nonthinkers then react with hate, prejudice, or revenge — emotions that underlie poor judgment and drive irrational behavior.

Wise people are aware of sensitive subjects and look at problems objectively. When talking about race, religion, politics, or any other controversial topic, they perceive others' positions not as threats but as differences of opinion. They stay lower on their Emotions Elevator than the person or people they are engaging.

Practice this skill by identifying race, gender, religion, politics, age, or other differences that send you up your Emotions Elevator. Review the wise ways and create strategies to help you handle difficult situations. Use your thinking skills to prevent or defuse a volatile situation you know has the potential for blowing up. "I know that you and I see things differently. Let's agree to disagree and talk about something else. Have you been to any good restaurants lately?"

Advance preparation lets your brain retrieve a "game plan" from your memory, giving you a greater chance to stop and think when confronted with highly emotional and volatile situations. With thinking skills, you learn to look at statements, people, or situations as different, not as right or wrong. This knowledge helps you respond thoughtfully and wisely when differences pose potential problems.

3. Assertive Communication

Assertive communication requires practice and the ability to understand another's point of view. Knowing how to respond assertively builds on all the skills you have learned in BrainWise. There are four communication styles: passive, aggressive, passive-aggressive, and assertive. Three of these — passive, aggressive, passive-aggressive — are triggered by emotions. The fourth method, assertive communication, uses the wise ways.

Passive communication involves putting aside your own feelings and needs to accept someone else's position. Triggered by fear, low self-esteem, and even anger, passive communication is an unconscious reaction to a situation in which you feel powerless.

Aggressive communication involves impulsive and volatile responses and is grounded in the strong emotions of threat and fear. The Lizard Brain moves seamlessly from fear of physical danger to fear of different cultures, fear of failure, fear of beliefs different from our own — fear of anything we perceive as a threat. The Lizard Brain responds the way it knows best — with aggression and hostility, which mimic a desire to "go for the throat."

Passive-aggressive communication also is fueled by feelings of perceived threat and fear. Often characterized by double messages, passive-aggressive communication may be difficult to detect at first because a benign or favorable remark is followed by viciousness or sarcasm.

There are many examples of passive-aggressive communication, from the spouse who tells her husband "not to go to any trouble," yet he knows that he had better bend over backwards to make sure she gets what she wants, to the coworker who says he will help on the project and does very little, but takes all of the credit.

Lizard Brain users are passive, aggressive, and passive-aggressive. Wizard Brain thinkers use **assertive communication,** a method that skillfully detects other people's faulty thinking and carefully gauges how to handle problems. This insight is honed by ongoing practice and application of the 10 Wise Ways. Assertive communicators access their Wizard Brain and the knowledge now stored in its memory banks.

Assertive communicators assess a situation before they make a statement. Their body language matches their verbal position. If passion is present, it is controlled and used effectively. They make their position clear, but without intimidation. Their statements are confident, intelligent, and fair.

Points of View (POV)

Good communicators recognize how their statements and actions affect other people. This concept was introduced in Wise Way #8 as Consequences Affecting Others (CAO) and is expanded here by applying it to communication.

Taking another person's point of view (POV) indicates higher-level thinking. This skill requires the wisdom not only to assess someone else's feelings but to consider how your position will affect her or him. This requires combining POV with effective communication techniques and all of the other wise ways, like Consequences Now and Later (CNL) and the Emotions Elevator. Wizard Brain users know they do not have to agree with the other person, but by considering the other person's position, they are able to respond wisely and with empathy.

POV helps you assess whether the person you are dealing with is using thinking skills. This knowledge helps you to understand other people's Lizard Brain behavior and to find nonthreatening ways of communicating with them. Your position as someone who does have thinking skills gives you an opportunity to effectively address other people's Lizard Brain responses.

When you learn and use the 10 Wise Ways, you have tools to be a highly effective communicator. Instead of reacting, your brain learns to connect to all the skills you have learned. POV is an important piece of this process.

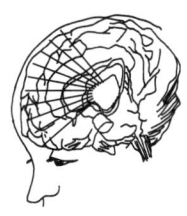

Build a Brain Connection

The more you practice applying and using your thinking skills, the more connections you build for your brain to access and the more efficient your brain becomes when using the knowledge you are accumulating.

• To practice using good nonverbal, verbal, and assertive communication styles, start by recognizing them in yourself and others.

Identify people who consistently show Lizard Brain responses and compare them with people who exhibit more thoughtful Wizard Brain responses. Make a mental note about what you have observed so your brain can file away the information for future reference.

• Make an effort to use "I" messages and to take other people's Points of View (POV).

AHA! Experience
[Jody, healthcare worker]

I HAVE HAD MANY AHA! EXPERIENCES WITH BRAINWISE. I can't say enough about its methods because they've changed my life and my son's life.

I am a single mom. Eli is my son and he was a big problem when he was in high school.

I won't go into details, but he did everything bad you can imagine, including flunking all of his classes because he skipped so much school. His last chance was attending an alternative high school. There he was assigned to a BrainWise course and had an awesome teacher.

I became interested in what he was learning when I started seeing some big changes in his behavior. Eli actually attended school! He made new friends at the school. He was happier. He came home from school and didn't stay out late at night. He didn't yell at me and seemed calmer. What was going on?

That's when I learned about his BrainWise class. He really liked his teacher and said his class was "full of kids like me." I asked him what he meant and he said, "Everyone thinks we're bad but we aren't. We've just been using our Lizard Brains." Even though I had not heard that term before, I knew exactly what he meant!

For the first time, Eli said that he was learning things that really worked and that he could use. He explained the Lizard Brain and Wizard Brain, Red Flags, the Constellation of

Support, and the Emotions Elevator. He continued to bring home information and began teaching me a mini version of the 10 Wise Ways. I learned about facts versus opinions, asking questions, identifying choices, CNL, CAO, goals, and communicating effectively.

I realized that much of my own behavior was Lizard Brain. I was pregnant with Eli when I got married. I divorced soon afterward and since then I have been in and out of relationships, some of them abusive. It's no wonder Eli had such a hard time, and I accept the blame. But when it was happening, I didn't know how to act any differently. My family and the people around me acted that way. It was the only way I knew. BrainWise changed all that.

I had never learned anything about the brain and knew nothing about thinking skills. It's like secret information. Maybe some people know it, but I bet that most people don't. The skills BrainWise teaches and the methods it uses helped Eli and me learn how to make better choices.

Eli graduated from high school and decided to join the army. He plans to go to college when he gets out. I am working part time as a nurse's aide and pursuing a nursing degree at our community college. Neither of us would have made good decisions like this before we learned thinking skills. I know it sounds strange, but if you have always had problems because you react instead of stopping to think, learning a new way to prevent problems is like a miracle.

But the story I want to tell is about Eli's class and the project they did during the second semester of the course. The kids were so excited about learning BrainWise that they actually petitioned for a second semester of the class.

What they did during that semester was absolutely amazing. They decided to write a play about the 10 Wise Ways and to use it to teach other kids thinking skills. They performed the play for other students at their school and also at a middle school many of them had attended.

The play was about a girl who was stuck in an abusive relationship and how she was able to make up her mind to leave it. Eli told me that he wasn't the only one who picked the subject; others in his class were familiar with family violence and abusive relationships.

Violence, they decided, was something they all had in common with many of their peers.

They called the play Whatcha Gonna Do? *It included several wonderful songs. I know their teacher deserves a lot of the credit for the songs, but he claimed, "Everyone helped." The play and the music really touched me. Here's one of the songs they wrote:*

STOP AND THINK

You've got to stop and think,
Use the 10 Wise Ways
Don't let the anger … or madness
Take you into a blaze.

You gotta stop and think.
You gotta take it down,
Get off the 10th floor
Get those feet on the ground.

Think about your dreams and
The choices you make.
Take a deep breath …
And let go of the hate.

You gotta stop and think,
Gotta heal yourself
And leave everyone's problems,
Put them up on a shelf.

Your soul becomes whole
When you let the pain go,
So take a deep breath …
And let the calm flow.

Written by Tim La Greca and the EGOS BrainWise class.

The play was great! Music and acting are such good ways to communicate. Eli was excited about writing the play. He played the role of the abusive boyfriend, and a teen mother in the class played his girlfriend. The play presents scenes between the girl and her boyfriend, leading up to her difficult decision to leave him. The kids in the cast performed their hearts out.

After each performance, Eli and the other actors sat on the stage and fielded questions from the audience. They were determined to expose others to the 10 Wise Ways. They used every communication skill they had learned to do so.

Thinking skills now are part of our lives and will be taught to my grandchildren and great-grandchildren.

BrainWise for Life

Our lives are not determined by what happens to us but by how we react to what happens.

— Unknown

When you ask, "What was I thinking?" you now know the answer. More importantly, you know how to change your Lizard Brain reactions and make wiser choices.

With practice, you will build brain connections and will be able to analyze problems so quickly that you won't even realize that you are thinking. You will make smart choices because:

Smart people use thinking skills to take responsibility for their behaviors — they don't lay blame or feel victimized. They use resources or people who can truly help them.

Smart people use thinking skills to make decisions based on facts. They ask the right questions, identify all their choices, and consider the Consequences Now, the Consequences Later, and the Consequences Affecting Others.

Smart people use thinking skills to recognize that setting goals and plans for action helps the brain focus on what needs to get done. Using "I" messages, engaging in assertive verbal and nonverbal behavior, and taking other people's points of view, Wizard Brain users skillfully communicate their positions and understand the positions of others.

It is easy to recognize when you are BrainWise: You become aware that you or others are using thinking, not emotion, to make choices and decisions. Remember, knowing the names of the Wise Ways does not mean that thinking skills have been mastered. It is a process that takes time and practice.

This book was written in response to parents and other adults who asked for a summary of the BrainWise program they could fit into their busy lives. They also asked "how long does it take to learn thinking skills?" There is no set answer, because learning varies with each individual. People with previous exposure grasp and use the Wise Ways more quickly than someone learning them for the first time. People who are serious and focused about learning them fare better than others who apply no or little effort.

How To Be BrainWise shows you that making smart choices has little to do with IQ and everything to do with replacing Lizard Brain reactions with Wizard Brain responses. Practice helps you internalize thinking skills — they become automatic and you apply them to all problems.

The last *AHA!* story about two special-needs students puts this process in perspective.

AHA! Experience

[Pat Austin, social worker and BrainWise instructor]

David looks younger than his age. He is 18 years old and enrolled in a regular high school with contained classrooms for severely developmentally disabled youth. His IQ is 50 and he had started experiencing incidents where he claimed to hear voices. He is friends with Ed, another disabled student with a slightly higher IQ. Both boys have been in my BrainWise class for three years.

With students in the regular high school, we spend 20–30 hours teaching BrainWise and another 30 hours reinforcing the skills. Special-needs students like David and Ed take much longer. I estimated that the other teachers and I had spent 300 contact hours teaching them. As this third year ended, I sometimes wondered if they had learned anything at all.

Although the boys take classes with other disabled students, they mix in the hallways between class periods with the regular high school students. During one of the passing periods, David was walking with Ed when he had a psychotic episode.

"Where is the green? Help me find the green!" he started crying over and over, hitting his forehead with his fist. Other students stared and backed off as Ed steered David to my office. They entered and David fell to the floor, twisting his body and pounding his forehead, crying, "I need the green, I can't find the green."

I tried to calm him. "You are safe, David. Take some deep breaths." In response he continued to wail, "Where is the green? I can't find the green!"

I did not know what he meant. "What is the green?" I asked. He was unable to reply and continued to moan, "I have to find the green."

Ed came to my rescue. "Mrs. Austin, you know! The green is his Wizard Brain. That's why we came to you!"

Now I knew! In our BrainWise class, each student receives a picture of the brain. They color the Lizard Brain red and the Wizard Brain green. When they learn a skill, they draw lines showing that they are making a connection to their Wizard Brain.

David desperately wanted to use his Wizard Brain! I discovered that he was hearing voices and seeing flying clocks. He thought "they" were coming to take the clocks and his brain. He was trying to find "the green" to help him deal with his delusions and came to me for help. I called his parents and doctor, who got him to a hospital where he was placed on new medication.

When David returned to school, I met with him and Ed to discuss the incident. We talked about the thinking skills both boys had used — recognizing red flags, seeking their constellation of support, lowering their Emotions Elevators, identifying choices, setting goals, and communicating effectively. Ed smiled broadly and said, "I used my Wizard Brain." David nodded in agreement and pointed to his forehead. "It's here," he said.

This incident gave me a chance to see the boys apply and use their thinking skills. I retired a month later and will treasure this episode as one of the most rewarding of my career. I continue to use BrainWise in my own life and teach it in my private practice.

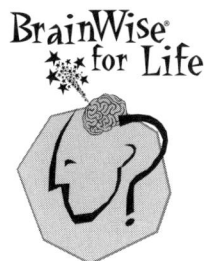

BrainWise for Life

BrainWise Checklists

We must become the change we want to see.
— Mahatma Gandhi

The last section of this book gives you reinforcement checklists we use in BrainWise classes, and workshops to help you remember to use Wizard Brain thinking. The checklists summarize the concepts used to describe and explain the thinking process.

Following the checklists is contact information so you can share your success stories with us. Those of us who use BrainWise look forward to hearing from you.

Checklist 1: Apply Thinking Skills to Your Problems

____ What type of thinking are you using — Wizard Brain or Lizard Brain?

____ What people or resources will help you manage or solve the problem?

____ What internal and external Red Flags signal that something is wrong?

____ What emotions do you feel and where are you on the Emotions Elevator? What can you do to lower your elevator? Are you lower on your elevator than the other person?

____ Are you able to separate facts from opinions?

____ Have you asked the right questions?

____ What are your choices?

____ What are the consequences (CNL and CAO) of each choice?

____ What is your goal? What is your plan to reach it?

____ Are you sending positive body messages? Using "I" messages? Respecting differences? Avoiding double messages? Making assertive statements? Taking others' POV?

Checklist 2: Apply Thinking Skills to Others' Problems *(Remember, many people have never learned skills to stop and think.)*

____ What type of thinking is the other person using — Wizard Brain or Lizard Brain?

____ What people or resources do they use to help them manage or solve the problem?

____ What external Red Flags signal that something is wrong?

____ What emotions are they showing and where are they on the Emotions Elevator? Are they doing anything to move lower on their elevator?

____ Do they separate facts from opinions?

____ Are they asking the right questions?

____ What are their choices? Do they think they have any choices?

____ What are the consequences (CNL and CAO) of each choice? Are they considering the consequences?

____ What is their goal? What are they doing to reach it?

____ How effective is their communication? Are they sending positive body messages? Do they use "I" messages? Respect differences? Avoid double messages? Make assertive statements? Take others' POV?

Checklist 3: Mastery of Thinking: Apply Thinking Skills to Your Problems and the Other Person's at the Same Time

_____ What type of thinking are you and the other person using — Wizard Brain or Lizard Brain?

_____ What people or resources will help you manage or solve the problem? What types of resources does the other person have and use?

_____ What internal and external Red Flags do you feel and see? Is the other person reacting to Red Flags?

_____ What emotions do you feel and where are you on the Emotions Elevator? What about the other person? What are you and the other person doing to lower your positions on the elevators? Are you on a lower floor than the other person? If not, why?

_____ Are you and the other person separating facts from opinions?

_____ Have you asked the right questions? Has the other person asked good questions?

_____ What choices do you and the other person have? Is the other person aware of his or her choices?

____ What are the consequences (CNL and CAO) of each choice? Is the other person aware of CNL and CAO?

____ What is your goal? Assess the other person's goal and compare it with yours. What is your plan to reach your goal using the information you have?

____ Are you able to communicate your position clearly? How does the other person react to your position? Are you sending positive body messages? What type of body messages is the other person sending? Are you using "I" messages? Respecting differences? Avoiding double messages? Making assertive statements? Is the other person able to communicate clearly? What kind of communication skills is the other person using?

Share Your Success

Let us know about your *AHA!* experiences. Log on to www.howtobebrainwise.com and go to Share Your Success, or mail your story to BrainWise, c/o Innisfree Press, P.O. Box 8375, Denver, CO 80201-8375.

TELL US ABOUT:

- Your *AHA!* experiences

- The *AHA!* experiences of others

- How using the 10 Wise Ways has helped you

- How using the 10 Wise Ways has helped someone else

- Useful teaching techniques

- How you have integrated the 10 Wise Ways into your life

- Unusual applications of the 10 Wise Ways

Stories that demonstrate the power of using thinking skills will be shared with others.

THANK YOU!

About the Author

Dr. Patricia Gorman Barry is the founder and director of a nonprofit agency formed to provide training and materials used to teach thinking skills. She is the author of *BrainWise for Grades K–5, BrainWise for Grades 6–12,* and *BrainWise One on One.* Her curricula are used by educators, youth advocates, and parents throughout the world.

Dr. Barry received a BA in sociology, a BS in nursing, and a Ph.D. in sociology from the University of Colorado, Boulder. She has worked with children, youth, and families as a health provider, educator, and researcher. She has trained thousands of instructors in schools, youth organizations, family service agencies, and businesses to teach thinking skills and integrate them into their classrooms, programs, and activities.

She lives with her family in Colorado.

All of us have the ability to use our brains better, but not everyone has the information and experience to do so. This book gives you language to describe and explain the thinking process.

The more you use your brain, the easier it is to make good choices. As you master thinking skills, remember that one of the highest levels of thinking is teaching what you know to others.

Glossary of Terms

Amygdala　　An almond shaped nucleus found in the brain's limbic system. The amygdala is found underneath the thalamus (or relay center) and plays a role in the memory for the emotional significance of experiences.

CAO　　Acronym for **C**onsequences **A**ffecting **O**thers.

CNL　　Acronym for **C**onsequences **N**ow and **L**ater.

Constellation of Support　　People and resources who help us solve problems from a supportive network around us, helping us stop and think about how to manage stressful situations.

Emotions Elevator　　An elevator in a ten-story building symbolizes the degree of intensity emotions can have, ranging from low and in-control (lower floors) to high and out-of-control (the top floors). Wizard Brain thinkers know how to lower their elevators or control their emotions by taking deep breaths, using control self-talk, redirecting their emotions, or using relaxation techniques.

Hypothalamus　　"Hypo" is Latin for "underneath." The hypothalamus sits underneath the brain's thalamus or relay center and controls the release of the "fight or flight" response.

IDC	Acronym for "**ID**entify all **C**hoices," a key concept needed to assess and analyze a problem before reacting.
Lizard Brain	Describes the section of the brain, also found in reptiles, that triggers the "fight or flight" reaction and other primitive instincts developed for survival.
POV	Acronym for **P**oint **O**f **V**iew, a learned response that promotes empathy and consideration of others. POV is a higher level thinking skill, requiring an individual to use multiple thinking processes simultaneously.
Prefrontal Cortex	The part of the brain, behind the forehead, containing complex intellectual functions that are activated by learning.
Red Flags	Internal and external signals that alert the brain to problem situations.
Thalamus	The part of the brain that receives information from the body's senses and acts as a relay center, sending the information directly to brain areas that evoke survival responses. If connections have been learned and developed, they will connect the thalamus to the cortex, the thinking or "wizard" brain will process them, creating a response based on rational thought and not emotions and impulse.

Wizard Brain   Term used to describe the prefrontal cortex
                            or area of the brain that processes complex
                            intellectual functions.

Bibliography

Barry, Patricia Gorman and Welsh, Marilyn (2006). The BrainWise curriculum: Neurocognitive development intervention program. In Daniel Romer (Ed.), *Adolescent Psychopathology and the Developing Brain*. New York: Oxford University Press.

Barry, Patricia Gorman (1996). *BrainWise for Grades 6-12*. Denver, CO: Innisfree Press.

Barry, Patricia Gorman (1998). *BrainWise for Grades K-5*. Denver, CO: Innisfree Press.

Barry, Patricia Gorman (1999). *BrainWise One-on-One for Counselors, Social Workers and Others Who Work Individually with Children and Youth*. Denver, CO: Innisfree Press.

Benson, H. (1975). *The relaxation response*. New York: Avon Books.

Burns, D. (1980). *Feeling good: The new mood therapy*. New York: New American Library.

Elias, M., Zins, J., Weissberg, R., Frey, K., Greenberg, M., Haynes, N., Kessler, R., Schwab-Stone, M., & Shriver, T. (1997). *Promoting social and emotional learning: Guidelines for educators*. Alexandria, VA: Association for Supervision and Curriculum Development.

Ellis, A. & Harper, A. (1975). *A new guide to rational living*. Hollywood, CA: Wilshire Book Company.

Gardner, H. (1993). *Multiple intelligences: The theory in practice*. New York: Basic Books.

Healy, J. (1998). *Failure to connect*. New York: Simon and Schuster.

Jenson, E. (2000). *Brain-based learning*. San Diego, CA: The Brain Store.

Kotulak, R. (1996). *Inside the brain: Revolutionary discoveries of how the mind works*. Kansas City, Kansas: Universal Press Syndicate Company.

LeDoux, J. (1996). *The emotional brain.* New York: Simon and Schuster.

Perry, B. (1997). *Using brain development findings to promote systemic change for children.* Paper presented at the BrainChild Initiative, Denver, CO: Colorado Children's Campaign.

Romer, Daniel. (2003). *Reducing adolescent risk: Toward an integrated approach.* Thousand Oaks, CA: Sage Publications.

Schwartz, J. & Begley, S. (2003). *The mind and the brain: Neuroplasticity and the power of mental force.* New York: Harper Collins.

Seligman, M. (1991). *Learned optimism.* New York: Alfred Knopf.

Steinberg, L. (1996). *Beyond the classroom: Why school reform has failed and what parents need to do.* New York: Simon and Schuster.

Sternberg, R. & Lubart, T. (1995). *Defying the crowd: Cultivating creativity in a culture of conformity.* New York: The Free Press.

Welsh, M., Friedman, S., & Spieker, S. (in press). Executive functions in developing children: Current conceptualizations and questions for the future. In Deborah Phillips, Kathleen McCartney (Eds.), *Handbook of early childhood development.* New York: Blackwell Publishers.